UNDERSTANDING THE
HOLOCAUST

Children of the Holocaust

Jenny MacKay

ReferencePoint
Press®

San Diego, CA

© 2016 ReferencePoint Press, Inc.
Printed in the United States

For more information, contact:
ReferencePoint Press, Inc.
PO Box 27779
San Diego, CA 92198
www.ReferencePointPress.com

LIBRARY OF CONGRESS CATALOGING-IN-PUBLICATION DATA

MacKay, Jenny, 1978- author.
  Children of the Holocaust / by Jenny MacKay.
    pages cm. -- (Understanding the Holocaust series)
  Includes bibliographical references and index.
  ISBN-13: 978-1-60152-838-4 (hardback)
  ISBN-10: 1-60152-838-8 (hardback)
  1. Jewish children in the Holocaust--Juvenile literature. 2. National socialism and youth--Juvenile literature. I. Title.
  D804.34.M35 2016
  940.53'18083--dc23

                                                                    2015009486

CONTENTS

IMPORTANT EVENTS OF THE HOLOCAUST

1937
Buchenwald concentration camp is established in east-central Germany.

1941
Germany invades the Soviet Union; the Germans massacre about one hundred thousand Jews, Roma (Gypsies), Communists, and others at Babi Yar in Ukraine; the United States declares war on Japan and Germany after Japan attacks Pearl Harbor.

1920
The Nazi Party publishes its 25-point program declaring its intention to segregate Jews from so-called Aryan society and to eliminate the political, legal, and civil rights of Germany's Jewish population.

1925
Adolf Hitler's autobiographical manifesto *Mein Kampf* is published; in it he outlines his political ideology and future plans for Germany and calls for the violent elimination of the world's Jews.

1940
The Warsaw ghetto—a 1.3 square mile (3.4 sq km) area sealed off from the rest of the city by high walls, barbed wire, and armed guards—is established in Poland.

1920 / 1934 1936 1938 1940

1918
The Treaty of Versailles, marking the formal end of World War I and a humiliating defeat for Germany, is signed.

1935
The Nuremberg Laws, excluding German Jews from citizenship and depriving them of the right to vote and hold public office, are enacted.

1939
Germany invades Poland, igniting World War II in Europe; in Warsaw, Jews are forced to wear white armbands with a blue Star of David.

1933
Hitler is appointed Germany's chancellor; the Gestapo is formed; Dachau concentration camp is established.

1938
Violent anti-Jewish attacks known as *Kristallnacht* (Night of Broken Glass) take place throughout greater Germany; the first *Kindertransport* (children's transport) arrives in Great Britain with thousands of Jewish children seeking refuge from Nazi persecution.

1942
The Nazi plan to annihilate Europe's Jews (the Final Solution) is outlined at the Wannsee Conference in Berlin; deportations of about 1.5 million Jews to killing centers in Poland begin.

1944
Allied forces carry out the D-Day invasion at Normandy in France; diplomats in Budapest offer protection to Jews.

1948
The State of Israel is established as a homeland for the world's Jews.

1946
The International Military Tribunal imposes death and prison sentences during the Nuremberg Trials.

1949
Argentina grants asylum to Josef Mengele, the notorious SS doctor who performed medical experiments on prisoners in Auschwitz.

1942   1944   1946   1948 / 1970

1943
Despite armed Jewish resistance, the Nazis move to liquidate ghettos in Poland and the Soviet Union; Denmark actively resists Nazi attempts to deport its Jewish citizens.

1960
In Argentina, Israeli intelligence agents abduct Adolf Eichmann, one of the masterminds of the Holocaust; he is brought to Israel to stand trial for crimes against the Jewish people.

1945
Allied forces liberate Auschwitz, Buchenwald, and Dachau concentration camps; Hitler commits suicide; World War II ends with the surrender of Germany and Japan; the Nuremberg Trials begin with war crimes indictments against leading Nazis.

1981
More than ten thousand survivors attend the first World Gathering of Jewish Holocaust Survivors in Israel; a similar gathering two years later in Washington, DC, attracts twenty thousand people.

1947
The UN General Assembly adopts a resolution partitioning Palestine into Jewish and Arab states; Holocaust survivor Simon Wiesenthal opens a center in Austria to search for Nazis who have evaded justice.

Children Deemed Less than Human

The late 1930s were a time of great uncertainty for the people of Europe. In Germany the rise to power of the Nazi Party allowed its leader, Adolf Hitler, to act on his belief that German society would be better off without certain kinds of people in it. Polish citizens, Roma (Gypsies), certain leaders of Catholic and other Christian churches, blacks, Jehovah's Witnesses, homosexuals, and persons with disabilities were all on Hitler's list of people he decided were unfit to be Germans. More than anyone else, however, he hated Jews. During the 1930s the Nazis began an aggressive campaign against Jews and other groups Hitler despised.

At first it seemed the Nazis meant only to force Jews and others on Hitler's list of undesirables out of German-occupied lands by making life unpleasant for them and their families. Jewish children, for example, were kicked out of schools and forbidden to play sports, visit parks, swim, go to the theater, or take part in other activities in which they previously had been welcomed. Such policies were only early signs of what was to come. By the late 1930s the Nazis' hostile behavior had turned violent, especially toward Jews. Austria, Denmark, Norway, the Netherlands, France, Belgium, Luxembourg, and part of Poland soon fell under Nazi control. In all of these places, Hitler ordered the Gestapo—the secret state police force that answered only to him—to round up unwanted people and either imprison or kill them.

Darkness Descends on Europe

Dread rippled across Europe in the wake of the Nazis' hatred-filled violence. In Switzerland, Chaim Weizmann, president of the World Zionist Organization that promoted Judaism, gave voice to the concerns of millions in 1939:

There is darkness all around us, and we cannot see through the clouds. . . . If, as I hope, we are spared in life and our work continues, who knows—perhaps a new light will shine upon us from the thick black gloom. . . . There are some things that cannot fail to come to pass, things without which our world cannot be imagined. The remnant shall work on, fight on, live on until the dawn of better days.[1]

Although his words encouraged Jews to stay focused on the future through the dark times Weizmann foresaw, millions truly began to fear for their lives.

Jewish parents were especially worried about the safety of their children, who were not exempt from the Nazis' primary goal of Jewish extermination—the total massacre of Jews. As Heinrich Himmler, head of the Schutzstaffel (SS) paramilitary corps during the Holocaust, told Nazi leaders during a secret speech in Poznan, Poland, in 1943, "I do not consider myself justified in eradicating the men—so to speak killing or ordering them killed—and allowing the avengers in the shape of the children to grow up for our sons and grandsons."[2] In other words, mercy was to be shown to no Jew during the Holocaust, not even the children.

Hunted Youth

With Nazis on a mission to destroy the so-called undesirables, no city or town in German-occupied areas was safe. Jews were captured, beaten, and killed for no offense other than being Jewish. SS soldiers had authority to raid homes, businesses, schools, churches, or any other building they believed might harbor Jews. Children, even infants, were treated just as harshly as adults. In fact, children were especially victimized, for a variety of reasons. Nazis aimed to eliminate young Jews before they grew up to have children of their own. Young Jews were called a useless burden on society. The Nazis' goals also included the torment of Jews in every way possible, and attacking Jewish children struck a unique kind of terror and grief. "Even in the most barbaric times, a human spark glowed in the rudest heart, and children were spared," wrote Holocaust historian Emanuel Ringelblum

Young prisoners, some wearing oversized striped uniforms, stare beyond the barbed wire of the Auschwitz death camp. Teenagers were sometimes spared because they could work, but few young children survived the Nazi genocide.

in 1942. "But the Hitlerian beast is quite different. It would devour the dearest of us, those who arouse the greatest compassion—our innocent children."[3]

Desperation drove Jewish parents and families to protect their children by any means possible. Their efforts resulted in a variety of difficult and tragic situations for children. Some were sent to live with strangers and forced to pretend they were not Jews. Others spent months to years of their childhood hiding in the wilderness or in dark, cramped city spaces like closets, basements, attics, or even sewers. However, even the frantic and often self-sacrificing efforts of parents and other caring adults to rescue or hide Jewish children could not save them all.

The number of children who died during the Holocaust is overwhelming. Of the 6 million Jews who were killed, 1.5 million were under age eighteen. Whereas an estimated 10 to 12 percent of Europe's adult Jewish population died during the Holocaust, about 30 percent of its Jewish children perished. Very young children and babies were targeted most of all. The fact that murderous atrocities were aimed disproportionately at the children is perhaps the Holocaust's most haunting legacy.

> "Even in the most barbaric times, a human spark glowed in the rudest heart, and children were spared. But the Hitlerian beast is quite different. It would devour the dearest of us, those who arouse the greatest compassion—our innocent children."[3]
>
> —Holocaust historian Emanuel Ringelblum.

Even when Germany's defeat in World War II brought an end to the Holocaust, the children's ordeal was not over. Countless young Jews who survived the Nazis' killing spree were orphaned and homeless. Most faced an uncertain future, wondering how and where they would live and whether they would ever know the fate of their parents and siblings. The Holocaust shattered the fragile innocence, security, and wonder of its most defenseless victims—the children.

CHAPTER ONE

Children in Hiding

As Hitler's plans to eradicate Europe's Jews became evident in the 1930s, some Jewish families were able to flee to safer places. This required money, however, something the Nazis took away from the Jews when they forbade them from working or doing business. Emigration also required, in many cases, express permission from the German government to leave the country. Such permission was often denied.

Many families who could not leave arranged to send at least their children to live with relatives, friends, or even acquaintances or total strangers who were willing to take in Jewish children, often in return for money. Historians estimate that between ten thousand and one hundred thousand Jewish sons and daughters were separated from their parents and hidden this way. Many children were assured that their family would be reunited once the war was over. Some were too young to understand such promises, but others spent years clinging to a hope that would never be realized. A majority of hidden children never saw their parents or siblings again.

Other families were determined not to split up and instead made plans to hide together at the first sign that the Gestapo was coming toward their town. The risk of evading Nazis this way was tremendous. Jews caught hiding could be killed on the spot, as could anyone who was believed to be helping them. Despite the dangers, hiding often proved to be a smart choice. Of the small number of Jewish children who survived the Holocaust, nearly all had been in hiding during the war.

Living in Disguise

Some Jewish children were able to blend in with non-Jews well enough to escape being noticed by the Nazis. Historians believe tens of thousands of children were sent to live in non-Jewish homes, orphanages, or convents during the Holocaust. Some caretakers pretended the children were family members. Others concocted somewhat believable stories to explain their presence, such as that they were servants or that they had been orphaned during a bombing raid. Children hidden this way spent weeks to years in a home that was not their own. Siblings often were not hidden together. People who agreed to look after Jews may have refused to accept more than one

Children enjoy a meal at an orphanage in Berlin before the start of World War II. Once the Nazis made clear their intentions toward Europe's Jews, some parents managed to send their children into hiding in non-Jewish orphanages and homes.

child to avoid raising suspicions among their neighbors. Many hidden children therefore suffered the heartache of being torn not only from their parents but from their brothers and sisters as well.

Hiding in someone else's family meant learning unfamiliar customs, obeying new rules, and sometimes feeling like a burden or a danger. Many hidden children also had to move multiple times as circumstances changed. Caretakers might have agreed to keep them only for a certain period of time and turned them out if their parents did not return for them. Some caretakers looked after Jewish children only as long as someone was paying them to do so, and when money ran out, so did their hospitality. This was not necessarily because host families were greedy or cruel. During the years of World War II, food was scarce in Europe and many people were very poor. Some families sent hidden children away because they simply could not afford to feed them anymore.

Nevertheless, moving from one home to another made hidden children feel displaced and unwanted. "The tensions were horrible," says Otto Verdoner, who was hidden by a Christian family during the Holocaust. "Things were just weird, weird, weird. . . . It is like you slam a door, everything disappears, you are somebody else. And you have no history, no antecedents, no memories, everything is wiped out."[4]

Double Identities

In addition to the emotional trauma of being separated from loved ones and familiar things, children who were old enough to know they were Jewish faced the difficult task of pretending they were not. Most hidden children were expected to pass as Christians, usually Catholics. They had to go to churches and learn customs contrary to their own faith. Most young people from Jewish families were used to attending synagogues, not churches, observing the Sabbath—or day of rest—from Friday to Saturday evening, and reading Judaism's most important text, the Torah, often in the Yiddish language. Pretending to be Catholic meant attending mass and observing the Sabbath on Sundays, studying and reciting prayers in Latin, and following the teachings of the Bible, including worshipping Jesus and the Virgin Mary. Christians observed different holidays than Jews, such as

A blessing is said as the candles are lit for the Jewish Sabbath. To avoid detection, young Jews who were sent to live with non-Jewish families had to abandon familiar beliefs and customs (such as the traditional Sabbath ritual).

Christmas instead of Hanukkah and Easter instead of Passover. They also ate different foods, such as pork, that were forbidden to Jews.

Jewish children sent to live in hiding with Christian families or in orphanages could not honor their own culture and heritage for fear that they would stand out as being Jewish. They had to be careful not to utter common phrases or blessings that could betray their true

Salvation in the Sewer

In June 1941 Nazis overtook the city of Lvov, Poland, home to 150,000 Jews. To avoid abuse or murder, a small group of Jews fled to the only safe place they could find—the sewers under the city's streets.

Among the refugees were the members of the Chiger family—seven-year-old Krystyna, her three-year-old brother, Pawelek, and their parents. For fourteen months the family hid with seven other people in the damp, putrid darkness of the underground sewers, kept alive by Polish sewer workers who brought them food and water every day. Krystyna and her family slept on sewage-covered stones. Their only source of light came from a carbide lamp. They spoke in whispers because of the constant fear that someone on the streets above might hear them. They shared the tunnels with rats that ate their bread. When it rained and the sewers flooded, Krystyna and Pawelek would have drowned in roiling human waste if their mother and father had not held them above the surface.

Krystyna later told about her experiences and the day they were finally freed. "I was so happy when I saw the sun, flowers and people," she said. "But Pawelek cried a lot. He wanted to go back to the sewer because he wasn't used to the light and he was afraid of people." Their story is a vivid example of the tortures children endured to survive the Holocaust.

Quoted in Anti-Defamation League Archive, "Children of the Holocaust: Krystyna's Story," 2001. http://archive.adl.org.

identity. "I had to lie, which was really a sin, no matter what religion I was supposed to belong to," says Chaya H. Roth, who had been hidden with a Catholic family in southern France. "When I was sinning was I Catholic or Jewish?"[5]

Hidden children sometimes feared that by pretending they were not Jews, they had turned their back on God. Others felt they were betraying their families by ignoring or even forgetting everything their parents and the leaders of their synagogue had taught them. This created conflict for young Jews who had been raised with strong spiritual beliefs and pride in their faith and heritage. "A slow transformation was taking place in me," says Nechama Tec, a Jew who survived the Holocaust by pretending to be Catholic while living with a Catholic family in Poland. "It was as if in certain circumstances I lost track of who I really was and began to see myself as a Pole. I became a double person, one private and one public."[6]

Hidden children had to leave behind physical traces of their Jewish upbringing, including favorite toys, familiar books, and even photographs of their loved ones. Such things might draw questions from suspicious passersby or visitors to the home. Some were even expected to change the way they spoke. Because many Jews spoke Yiddish at home, their German, Polish, or other language was often accented, meaning their speech could potentially give away their true identity. "I knew when to be quiet, what not to say, and how to avoid attracting attention," Olga Kirshenbaum Weiss recalled of her days in hiding. "I had been given a false, non-Jewish name, and I fully understood, even at that early age, that I must never make the mistake of acknowledging my real name."[7]

> "A slow transformation was taking place in me. It was as if in certain circumstances I lost track of who I really was and began to see myself as a Pole. I became a double person, one private and one public."[6]
>
> —Nechama Tec, a hidden child.

In order to further protect hidden children, some families told everyone that the child was mute or was mentally handicapped so that no one would prod him or her with questions. Such lies were meant to protect Jewish children. Nonetheless, it was humiliating for them to have to pretend they were unintelligent or mute and to silently endure the teasing and ridicule that often followed.

The Struggle to Feel Loved

The penalty for protecting a Jewish child from the Nazis was harsh; discovery often meant death. Many of the people who took this risk therefore set strict rules for their Jewish wards, punishing them for doing or saying anything that might signal to others that the family was trying to hide a Jew. So much energy was focused on avoiding detection that foster parents sometimes overlooked the importance of being kind and loving. This often led to strained relationships between Jewish children and the adults who hid them. Strong-willed children who experienced strict discipline sometimes rebelled and misbehaved. In the absence of affection, quieter children could be sullen or withdrawn. The caretakers, in turn, often felt that their Jewish charges were ungrateful for the sacrifices being made on their behalf and became harsher and less understanding.

> "I knew when to be quiet, what not to say, and how to avoid attracting attention. . . . I fully understood, even at that early age, that I must never make the mistake of acknowledging my real name."[7]
>
> —Olga Kirshenbaum Weiss, a hidden child.

As a very young child, Holocaust survivor Bernadette Gore was sent to live in a French village with a woman she remembers as being cruel, although as an adult she came to understand things from a different point of view. "At the time there was such heavy fighting around there. . . . If they had come to her and I had given the game away, they would have shot her," she says. "So I suppose she had to be very severe with me, and she had to efface from my mind anything to do with my past."[8] Even understanding the danger of their situation did not always soften children's feelings that the people who looked after them did not love or even like them. Life in hiding was at best a challenging experience for most children. At worst, it was intolerable. Some hidden children were forced to work as household servants or farmhands. Others endured physical, emotional, or sexual abuse from the adults who took them in. Some young people ran away from their hiding homes, preferring the risk of being captured by the Nazis to living in a home where they felt mistreated or unwanted.

Taking Refuge

Not all Jewish parents tried, or were able, to send their children to live with others during the Holocaust. Some parents did not know anyone who was not Jewish or who was willing to take in their child. Many Jewish families were too poor to be able to pay anyone to look after their children or had too many children to place them all in safe homes. Some families just preferred to stay together. These families were forced to find different ways to hide in an effort to survive.

Jewish children who went into hiding with their parents and siblings usually did so in a hurry. The Gestapo typically arrived with little warning other than the sound of boots marching up the street, voices shouting, and fists pounding on doors. Frightened children were told to be silent and to hurry as their parents pushed or pulled them through windows or back doors. They fled to abandoned buildings or other places they hoped the Nazis would not search.

Some families had worked out specific hiding places, building hidden rooms or digging out caves with carefully disguised entrances. When Nazi forces came, families sneaked into the attics, basements, or tunnels they had created. Often spaces that would have been cramped with only one family became a living space for additional relatives, friends, or even total strangers who were desperate for a refuge.

A hole cut into the brick wall of this house in the Netherlands shows a cramped hiding place used by Jews during the Holocaust. The entrance was through the bottom shelf of the linen closet.

Starving in Darkness

Living conditions in most of these hiding places were miserable. For necessities such as food and water, families in hiding often depended on non-Jews who knew they were there. The hidden families could only hope that their helpers would continue to bring supplies and not betray them to the Nazis. There was rarely enough food or water to go around, much less to satisfy the appetites of growing children.

In addition to the lack of food, sanitation was a problem. Bathing was out of the question in most hiding places, as was disposing of human waste. In some hideouts, a person who brought food and water also brought a bucket for the hiders to use, but for many there was no one to cart away waste. Infants and toddlers too young to be potty trained posed an additional problem because diapers were difficult to come by and impossible to wash.

Filthy living conditions put the health of everyone at risk, but small, frail children especially struggled to fend off disease. Skin infections were common among hidden children during the Holocaust, as were illnesses of the digestive tract. People, especially children, who endured long periods with little food were inclined to overeat when sporadic meals were provided. "People died by eating too much," says Ilana Rosen, who survived the Holocaust in Hungary as a child. "They started to eat a lot, out of hunger. . . . They got diarrhea and died. My sister took care of us. If it weren't for her, we too would have died."[9]

Not only were most hiding spaces overcrowded, filthy, cramped, and unhealthy, but many also were cut off from sunlight or fresh air. Nazi soldiers or even neighbors willing to turn in hiding Jews might see hiders through windows or other openings. Some of the most effective hiding places therefore lacked any view to the outside. In fact, many hiding places, such as underground caves or secret compartments in basements or attics, were nearly or completely dark all the time. Some young children who lived through the hiding experience had no recollection of sunlight when they finally emerged.

Childhood in Silent Spaces

The need for silence was especially important during hiding, and this complicated the experience even more for children. Many families hid in abandoned buildings. A thump, a voice, or a whimper might

The Diary Read Around the World

In 1942 twelve-year-old Anne Frank slipped into hiding in an office building in Amsterdam to evade capture by Nazis. Anne spent the next two years crammed into small rooms with her parents, older sister, and four other Jews. Her father had given her a diary, anticipating that his lively and outspoken daughter would need an outlet during the long months of hiding. Anne avidly chronicled all the details of the experience but also her many musings about life. Her diary was silenced after August 1, 1944, when Nazis found the family and sent them to concentration camps. Anne, her sister, and her mother died there. Only Anne's father survived. In 1947 he had portions of her diary published. Eventually translated into sixty-seven languages, it has become the most famous first-person account of the Holocaust.

Many of Anne's thoughts that were shocking or portrayed anger or irritability were not included in the originally published diary. In 1996 Anne's cousin, Buddy Elias, had the complete, uncensored diary published. It was 30 percent longer than the original version and included every word Anne wrote during her time in captivity, the uplifting and the pessimistic alike. "It shows her in a truer light," he says of the full, uncut version. "People try to make a saint out of her and glorify her. That she was not. She was an ordinary, normal girl with a talent for writing." Her unabridged diary provides a well-rounded view of the Holocaust's effects on a bright young mind.

Quoted in Marianne MacDonald, "The Things That Anne Was Really Frank About," *Independent* (London), October 22, 1996. www.independent.co.uk.

be heard by passersby outside who would give away the location of the hiding place. Ingrid Epstein Elefant, a Holocaust survivor who was forced into hiding as a child, recalls "the long black days of dense and deafening silence." She continues, "No radio played my favorite songs. . . . 'Shshshsh,' said Oma [Grandmother] when I hummed a little tune. 'Shshsh,' said Onkel (Uncle) Leo if I spoke above a whisper."[10] Silence is unnatural for children, but young Jews hiding in such places learned to endure life without talking, laughing, or singing, much less running around or playing games.

Parents of babies often faced an especially terrible dilemma. A crying baby could give away the location of the entire group. If an infant could not be quieted, the mother or father usually had to leave the hiding place with the baby and risk being captured or kill the baby so that it would stop making noise. "This was a war, a terrible war, a war of survival," says Holocaust survivor Sonia Bielski. "Mothers and fathers [were] killing the children. . . . The [children were] hungry and they were crying so they killed them."[11]

Sacrificing Youth to Stay Alive

Often trapped in darkness and forbidden to speak, Jewish children who lived in hideouts missed out on activities necessary for growing up and developing normally. Whereas other kids their own age were playing games and sports, raising pets, and going to school, hidden young people missed out on all the joys and experiences of a normal childhood. Instead, hunger, lice, illness, boredom, loneliness, and depression filled their seemingly endless days. Most Jews who went into hiding this way had fled suddenly, leaving behind treasured keepsakes and even changes of clothing that would fit them as they grew. "As a four-year-old, I felt naked, exposed, vulnerable, deprived, angry, and confused," says Clemens Loew, who survived the Holocaust in Poland. "I'd just been literally stripped of all my toys and possessions."[12]

> "We are the children without a childhood. We are the children who aged instantly, overnight."[13]
>
> —Robert Krell, a hidden child.

Surviving these conditions was an extraordinary feat of determination and willpower. Spending even a few days this way would be unimaginable to most people today, but during the Holocaust Jews in hiding endured weeks, months, or even years in very challenging conditions. Deprived of nutrition, cleanliness, privacy, dignity, education, and freedom, children who successfully hid from Nazis during the Holocaust emerged with their lives but at the cost of their youth. "We are the children without a childhood," says Holocaust survivor Robert Krell. "We are the children who aged instantly, overnight."[13]

CHAPTER TWO

Children in Captivity

In 1940, as Jews across Nazi-occupied Europe scrambled for hiding places, new construction projects were under way in the Polish cities of Warsaw and Lodz, both home to many Jews. In Lodz, Nazi workers erected fences of barbed wire around a group of abandoned factories. In Warsaw, home to the most Jews of any city in Europe and one of the world's major centers of Jewish life and culture, German workers erected 10-foot (3 m) walls topped with barbed wire to seal off a section of the city. These were among thousands of similar neighborhoods, or ghettos, created in other German-controlled cities, and their construction was a sinister precursor of dreadful things to come.

Prior to 1940 some Jewish parents had underestimated the Nazis' capacity for cruelty or had believed their government would protect their families from mistreatment, even if Germans occupied the country. Other parents had recognized warning signs of impending danger but had lacked the money or resources to send their children out of harm's way. Whatever situations the persecuted families faced, one thing became clear by the late 1930s: The Nazi government meant to eliminate all of them. The creation of prison-like places to house them was all part of a massive plan for dealing with so-called undesirables, right down to the tiniest child.

Urban Imprisonment

Isolating unwanted people was the first major step in the Nazis' plan to standardize the German population. SS forces scoured German-occupied areas to round up families targeted for removal. The soldiers often received help from local citizens who themselves disliked Jews, Gypsies, or others and were eager to point out where these neighbors lived. Children unknowingly helped the Nazis carry out these roundups too. Threats that children would be hurt made parents more likely to do as they were told, which helps explain why hundreds of thousands of Jews and other persecuted people in German-occupied

Ghettos, Camps, and Killing Centers, 1942

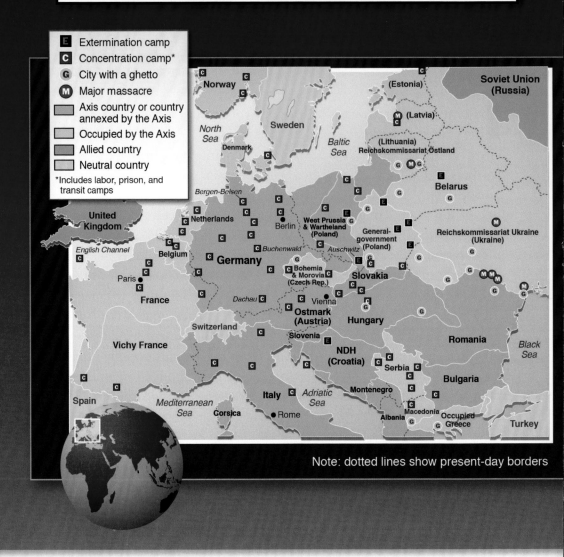

E Extermination camp
C Concentration camp*
G City with a ghetto
M Major massacre
[ ] Axis country or country annexed by the Axis
[ ] Occupied by the Axis
[ ] Allied country
[ ] Neutral country
*Includes labor, prison, and transit camps

Norway
North Sea
Sweden
Denmark
Baltic Sea
(Estonia)
(Latvia)
(Lithuania)
Reichskommissariat Ostland
Soviet Union (Russia)
United Kingdom
Bergen-Belsen
Netherlands
Berlin
West Prussia & Wartheland (Poland)
General-government (Poland)
Belarus
Reichskommissariat Ukraine (Ukraine)
English Channel
Belgium
Buchenwald
Auschwitz
Germany
Paris
France
Dachau
Vienna
Ostmark (Austria)
Bohemia & Moravia (Czech Rep.)
Slovakia
Hungary
Switzerland
Vichy France
Slovenia
NDH (Croatia)
Serbia
Romania
Black Sea
Spain
Mediterranean Sea
Corsica
Italy
Rome
Adriatic Sea
Montenegro
Albania
Macedonia
Occupied Greece
Bulgaria
Turkey

Note: dotted lines show present-day borders

lands went peacefully when taken from their homes. Parents were trying not to give the brutal SS soldiers any added reason to abuse their children.

Jews far outnumbered any other group the Germans apprehended, and they were forced to move into densely crowded and closely guarded areas of concentration such as the parts of Warsaw and Lodz that had been surrounded by walls and fences of barbed wire. Within the walls of these ghettos the SS controlled, stole from, humiliated, and abused captives in almost any way imaginable. The ghettos sealed Jews off from outside sources of help and all but eliminated the possibility of escape. Although the Nazis led outsiders to believe ghettos were really just ethnic neighborhoods for Jews, they much more closely resembled massive urban prisons. Ghetto entrances and exits were few, and these were defended by armed guards. Anyone who attempted to escape—even a child—risked being shot and killed.

Jewish children forced into one of these neighborhoods led a punishing existence. Ghetto police and Nazi guards were as cruel to children as to everyone else, and once trapped in the ghettos, parents could do little to protect their families. The lives of ghetto children were filled with suffering and loss, their futures determined by the merciless whims of the SS and the ghetto police. Vulnerable, fragile, and often helpless, children in the ghettos faced a relentless struggle to survive.

Cold, Crowded, and Underfed

Overcrowding was a signature feature of ghettos. In Warsaw four hundred thousand Jews eventually lived in an area of just 1.3 square miles (3.4 sq km)—the approximate equivalent of cramming the entire population of Oakland, California, or Omaha, Nebraska, into New York City's Central Park. Most ghetto children slept several people to a bed or mattress in run-down buildings that lacked reliable sources of heat. Many ghettos also lacked flushing toilets or sewage systems, so residents were forced to relieve themselves on sidewalks or in the halls and stairwells of buildings. Ghetto orphans spent their days huddled on sidewalks that were covered with human waste.

The Nazis often took warm clothing and shoes away from children when they arrived at the ghetto, forcing many to suffer through the chilly winter months dressed in little more than rags. Emanuel Ringelblum provided aid to residents of the Warsaw ghetto and wrote the following in his notes of the experience in 1941: "The most fearful sight is that of the freezing children. Little children with bare feet, bare knees, and torn clothing, stand dumbly in the street weeping."[14] Exposure to wet or snowy weather and freezing temperatures took the lives of many children in the ghettos.

Not only were ghetto children often deprived of adequate clothing and comfortable living spaces, many were plagued by hunger and thirst. The youngest children suffered from hunger more than almost anyone else. The Nazis considered older children and teens to be valuable and forced many of them into unpaid working arrangements. Children who were too young to be useful and were left behind in the ghettos posed an expensive problem, for they needed to be fed. The Nazis were reluctant to provide meals, calling the children *nutzlose esser*, "useless eaters."[15]

Nazi overseers of ghetto neighborhoods restricted the amount of food allocated to young children even more severely than the amount given to teenagers and adults. Ghetto children often existed on two hundred or fewer calories a day. (Modern nutritional guidelines recommend one thousand calories a day for children ages two to three, twelve hundred to fourteen hundred calories for ages four to eight, and sixteen hundred to more than two thousand calories for ages nine through eighteen). For a child, an entire meal in a ghetto might have

Filthy and hungry, Jewish children sit on the ground with empty food bowls in the Warsaw ghetto in 1941. Ghetto residents endured hunger, disease, and cold.

consisted of a partial potato or onion. Children became so thin that the bones of their knees and elbows sometimes broke through their dry, fragile skin.

Constant thirst accompanied the relentless hunger. The run-down and poorly maintained neighborhoods often lacked running water, so drinking water was provided in buckets many people had to share. Importing drinking water to ghetto residents was both costly and time-consuming, so water, like food, was strictly rationed. Water for bathing was even scarcer than drinking water, and filth led to illness for ghetto children. The Nazis' ultimate goal was to eliminate ghetto residents, so medical care for dirty, underfed, sick children in these places was not a priority. Medicines were rare or even impossible for residents to obtain. Ghetto walls stood between the captive children and the basic things they needed to survive.

Smuggling for Survival

Adult residents of the ghettos attempted to make life better for the children, but they could do little to improve the living conditions. Anything of potential value—including books and toys—was usually confiscated upon entering the ghetto. Most ghettos also had rules against educating Jewish children. There were no schools, parks, or playgrounds. Young people who attended makeshift schools, along with the adults who taught them, were in constant danger of being caught and punished or even killed. "Jewish children learn in secret," reads a December 1941 entry from the diary of Chaim Kaplan, who organized a secret school in the basement of his home in the Warsaw ghetto. "They hide their books and notebooks between their trousers and their stomachs, then button their jackets and coats."[16]

So desperate were ghetto residents for basic supplies for the children—food and medicine but also things like notebooks and paper—that a secret market developed for items to make life tolerable. Smugglers—often children because they were small, fast, and agile and thus could squeeze through cracks in walls and into and out of the sewers—worked throughout the ghetto, bringing in various commodities that could improve or even save lives. "Little kids wore coats with hundreds of pockets sewn into the inside," says Max Glauben, who at twelve years old became a child smuggler in the Warsaw ghetto in 1941. "We went on raids for sugar, beans, and other things in the middle of the night. It might not have been honorable, but we did that in order to save many lives inside the ghetto."[17] It was a risky occupation. Those caught smuggling could be whipped or killed. Still, the smugglers persisted. In some ghettos an estimated 80 percent of the food people ate came from smuggling, and this was also the only way to obtain toys or other amenities.

Parents in the ghettos often went to great lengths to get a share of the smuggled resources for their children. They became desperate to obtain things, even at the cost of other children's happiness. "The tragedy of the Holocaust was that in the limited instances when people had an opportunity to do certain things, often there was competition for survival,"[18] says Ervin Staub, a childhood survivor of the Holocaust. The desperate circumstances of the ghettos forced children to be part of a daily battle to live.

> "The tragedy of the Holocaust was that in the limited instances when people had an opportunity to do certain things, often there was competition for survival."[18]
>
> —Ervin Staub, a child survivor.

Orphaned ghetto children who had no assistance from adults fared especially poorly in this atmosphere of relentless competition; as a result, they were less likely than other children to live through the ordeal. Unfortunately, those who did survive the ghettos often went on to still further torment. The ghettos were only one step in the Nazis' plan to eliminate people they had deemed as threats to their ideal society.

Camps of Doom

The precise number of children who died in ghettos in the 1930s and 1940s is unknown, but historians believe tens of thousands to hundreds of thousands of young lives ended in those miserable conditions. Deadly as ghettos were, however, they proved inefficient in the Nazis' ultimate goal of exterminating people they despised. Beginning in 1933, Nazis began to take groups of ghetto residents to train stations and crowd them into cattle cars destined for locations where killing could be drastically accelerated.

Starvation's Lifelong Victims

Children forced into ghettos, concentration camps, or hiding during the Holocaust rarely received enough to eat. Many became very thin and frail. Their weakened and malnourished bodies struggled to fend off diseases that ran rampant in many camps and ghettos, where there was little to no medical care.

Not only did most children receive far fewer calories than they needed to grow normally and maintain healthy immune systems, but their restricted diets also did not contain the variety of vitamins and minerals they needed. Vitamin deficiencies caused many additional health problems for children of the ghettos. A lack of vitamin A affected vision, resulting in night blindness. A vitamin B_3 deficiency caused pellagra, the symptoms of which included diarrhea, dermatitis (soreness, swelling, and blistering of the skin), and confusion. The absence of iron-rich foods led to anemia, a blood condition that causes fatigue, shortness of breath, and pale skin. Limited calcium and vitamin D caused rickets, a disease that softens and weakens the bones and leads to bowed legs.

Those who survived the Holocaust as children eventually ate normally again, but in many cases they developed health problems that stayed with them throughout their entire lives. Bone diseases and chronic bone pain, for example, are more common among people (especially women) who endured the Holocaust as children than among people who did not. The effects of the starvation that children faced during the Holocaust persist in survivors even today.

Children joined grown men and women in these dark and crowded traveling compartments. There were usually two buckets in each cattle car—one that held drinking water and one to collect the passengers' waste during the journey. The odor was atrocious, and with only tiny windows to provide light or fresh air, passengers felt smothered and claustrophobic. Children, especially, were prone to panic and fear aboard the cattle cars. Denise Holstein, who at age seventeen looked after nine orphaned children who were deported on one of these journeys, later told of her experience aboard the train. "By evening, when we had to put all those children to bed in the pitch-dark, the screams began. . . . The children were hot, they were thirsty, and we were running out of air." To console them, she said, "we sang songs of travel and hope."[19]

Hope was to be short-lived for the ill-fated children of these journeys. The train tracks often ended right at the gates of a much different kind of holding center than the ghettos—a concentration camp, which was to be the final destination in the lives of most of the passengers on the trains. Children, especially, were not destined to live long in the camps. The Nazis had decided that mothers with young children, women carrying or accompanied by children, and children traveling alone should be eliminated as soon as possible. Many children who were sent to the camps were murdered within as little as two hours from the moment they stepped off the train.

A trainload of Jews—mostly women and children—arrives at the Auschwitz death camp. Mothers and young children were often sent to their deaths soon after they arrived.

The few children who survived the day of their arrival were forced to dress in the standard striped prisoner garb, their heads were shaved, their forearm was tattooed with an identification number, and they were sent to live in barracks that were even more crowded than the ghettos. Food was at least as scarce as within the ghettos, and medical care was usually nonexistent unless an adult prisoner with medical training happened to live in the same barrack or nearby. Here, unlike in the ghettos, smuggling was not a source of needed goods like food and medicine because most concentration camps were built far outside of cities, and their fences were rigged to electrocute anyone who touched them. With no way to import desperately needed items, young prisoners were at the total mercy of their Nazi captors.

"By evening, when we had to put all those children to bed in the pitch-dark, the screams began."[19]

—Denise Holstein, a teenage survivor.

Hidden Experiments

Built in relatively isolated locations, concentration camps made it easier for the SS forces to carry out their terrible treatment of prisoners—including the murder of millions of children—without drawing much attention from outsiders. The Nazis nevertheless took measures to mask the horrible conditions within concentration camps and to convince the rest of the world that prisoners, especially children, lived well and were even happy. Young prisoners were forced to smile for photographs sent to newspapers as proof that camp life was pleasant. At Auschwitz in Poland, the largest, deadliest, and most notorious of all the concentration camps, Nazis even built a playground. They made sure it was easily visible from outside the camp to give the illusion that the children inside were treated well. Children did not use this equipment, however. Most of the few children who survived past the day of their arrival at Auschwitz had been chosen instead for a sinister purpose, one that left them in no condition to play.

In April 1942, a year after Auschwitz was opened, a doctor named Josef Mengele arrived there. Mengele had a keen interest in genetics and medical experiments. Before going to Auschwitz, he had been limited in the experiments he could conduct on living people due to

The Holocaust in Children's Literature

Maurice Sendak (1928–2012), the author of many famous and award-winning children's picture books, including *Where the Wild Things Are*, was born in New York City to Jewish immigrants from Poland. Although he grew up safely out of reach of the Nazis, many of his relatives in Poland died in concentration camps, including cousins his own age. The Holocaust affected Sendak deeply as a child and throughout his life. "I was made to feel guilty all the time," he said. "It constantly made me feel that I was shamelessly enjoying myself while they (cousins) were being cooked in an oven."

As an adult, Sendak channeled some of his feelings into his picture books. Many of his young characters escape from their everyday world into fantastic, make-believe settings, as children trapped in ghettos or concentration camps might have wanted to do. One of Sendak's works, a play titled *Brundibar*, has direct ties to children of the Holocaust. Its title character is a bully who tries to prevent two poor children from getting milk for their sick mother. Hundreds of kids band together to help the siblings by driving Brundibar from town. In the end, however, Brundibar is not completely defeated and vows to come back another day. The foreboding conclusion reflects Sendak's fears that the type of thinking that inspired the Holocaust could one day resurface and afflict the world again.

Quoted in Bill Moyers, "Maurice Sendak: *Where the Wild Things Are*," *Now on PBS*, March 12, 2004. www.pbs.org.

medical ethics. It was illegal in Germany and elsewhere to do anything to patients that could harm their health. At Auschwitz, however, there was no such thing as ethics when it came to prisoners. Thousands of new research subjects arrived at the camp daily, and Mengele was able to choose whomever he wished to use for his experiments.

Many of Mengele's chosen ones were children—especially twins, who were genetically identical and therefore fascinated him. Mengele and his twenty-two-person medical team carried out a wave of dreadful experiments on children, from injecting them with experimental chemicals and deadly illnesses like typhoid to electrocuting them, exposing them to radiation, and conducting horrific surgeries. Eva Mozes Kor lived at Auschwitz as a child, and at age ten she became a victim of Mengele's experiments. Decades later she still vividly recalls the experimental treatments she endured in the camp:

> Three times a week, both of my arms would be tied to restrict the blood flow, and they took a lot of blood from my left arm, on occasion enough blood until I fainted. At the same time that they were taking blood, they would give me a minimum of five injections in my right arm. After one of these injections, I became extremely ill, and Dr. Mengele came in the next morning with four other doctors. He looked at my fever chart, and he said, laughing sarcastically, "Too bad. She's so young. She has only two weeks to live."[20]

Eva, who had a twin sister, did not know what illness had been injected into her body, but she fought through it for her own sake and for her sister's. "I would keep telling myself, 'I must survive,'" she says. "Would I have died, my twin sister Miriam would have been rushed immediately to Mengele's lab, killed with an injection to the heart, and then Mengele would have done the comparative autopsies. That is the way most of the twins died."[21]

"Dr. Mengele came in the next morning with four other doctors. He looked at my fever chart, and he said, laughing sarcastically, 'Too bad. She's so young. She has only two weeks to live.'"[20]

—Eva Mozes Kor, a child survivor of Auschwitz.

Being chosen for medical experimentation at Auschwitz at first seemed a blessing, not a curse. The children Mengele chose as study subjects not only avoided death immediately after their arrival but were often given special treatment—extra food and sweets but also nice clothing and playthings. Typically these items were taken from other children who had not survived their first day in the camp. Mengele pampered his young research subjects so that they would go with him trustingly to his laboratory when the time for experimentation came. Mengele's victims often paid for the pampering with their lives.

The Nazis imprisoned helpless young people in unlivable conditions and subjected them to starvation and experimentation as part of their plan to eliminate Jews and other so-called undesirables from Europe. Often orphaned or separated from their parents and lacking the means to fend for themselves, the vast majority of children forced into ghettos or across the gates of concentration camps never came out.

CHAPTER THREE

The Killing of Children

Adults trapped within ghettos and concentration camps developed strategies to help children endure the wretched conditions. Some, for instance, gave away their own rations of food and necessities in the hope that at least the youngest prisoners might live to see the end of the war and of Nazi brutality. Such compassion and sacrifice for the sake of the children frustrated the Nazis, who wished to exterminate both children and adults as quickly as possible. The Nazi regime realized it needed faster and more efficient ways to bring about death than just waiting for starvation and disease to run their course. By 1941 Nazi leaders had changed tactics in their genocidal war. They had decided to simply murder their victims outright, paying no heed to their age.

Harbingers of Death

In 1941 Hitler reorganized his military forces to include battalions of soldiers known as the Einsatzgruppen (German for "Task Forces"), whose entire job was to murder unwanted people, especially Jews. Einsatzgruppen units, each consisting of five hundred to nine hundred soldiers, were assigned to areas the German military was overtaking by force. The Einsatzgruppen followed on the heels of the regular army with the singular purpose of sweeping an area, finding all Jews living or hiding there, and killing them immediately.

People already living in ghettos were easy targets. They were centered where the Einsatzgruppen could find them easily, and the ghetto walls made escape attempts futile. Furthermore, after living for weeks, months, or years in the dreadful conditions of the ghetto, many captives—especially children—were too weak, sick, and weary to fight back or to run from the Einsatzgruppen. The Nazi forces conducted roundups by cordoning off a specific block or area of a ghetto, collecting victims, and ordering them to go outside in groups. To avoid causing panic, the soldiers regularly lied to their captives, assuring them that they were simply being relocated, often to places that sounded much more pleasant than the ghetto.

Having been cut off from news sources while living in the ghettos, many victims were unaware of the Nazis' real intentions. Even those who suspected the fate that awaited them knew that struggling would just make things worse for their loved ones or companions. "How could they have resisted?" Holocaust survivor Eve Nussbaum Soumerai and history professor Carol D. Schulz ask in the book they cowrote. "They possessed no weapons and were trying to protect their children. The guns were all on the other side."[22] Children, like adults, were afraid of the soldiers, the shouts, and the cries during roundups. However, although frightened and often tearful, they generally took cues from the parents or other adults around them and did what the Einsatzgruppen told them to do.

Frightened Jewish families surrender to Nazi soldiers in the Warsaw ghetto in 1943. Nazi units known as Einsatzgruppen periodically rounded up and shot to death Jews in the ghettos and then dumped their bodies in mass graves.

Hopeless obedience to the Einsatzgruppen's orders is captured in photographs taken of the child victims of these mobile killing squads. The typical course of events, once the Einsatzgruppen had swept a ghetto, town, or neighborhood, was to march captives to a ditch or a pit intended as a mass grave. There, victims were ordered to undress and were lined up alongside the pit or, in some cases, forced to lie facedown among the bodies already in it before they were shot. For the Einsatzgruppen, this practice eliminated the need to carry bodies to mass graves. For the victims, including children whose last vision in life was the naked, dead bodies of their family members or the other people they knew, the horror is unimaginable.

No victims of these killing-squad murders had a chance to write down what they felt in the final moments, but photographs taken of children in this desperate situation reflect a practice so appalling that it was deemed inhuman by many who witnessed or took part in it. August Häfner, who served as a first lieutenant in the SS, testified during a war crimes trial after the war about the shooting of children: "The children were taken down from the tractor. They were lined up along the top of the grave and shot so that they fell into it. . . . I shall never forget the scene throughout my life. I find it very hard to bear."[23]

> "They were lined up along the top of the grave and shot so that they fell into it . . . I shall never forget the scene throughout my life. I find it very hard to bear."[23]
>
> —August Häfner, first lieutenant in the SS.

The Evolution of Murder

The killing squads eliminated Jews much more quickly than starvation and disease in the ghettos had been able to do, but Nazi leaders became concerned about the emotional toll of all that killing—not on the victims but on the killers themselves. "Apparently for all but the basest members of the Einsatzgruppen, the bloody scenes led to significant psychological reactions," says historian Helmut Langerbein. Shooting children, in particular, proved especially difficult for some soldiers. "A young officer who had participated in the shooting of children for the first time started screaming for his mother,"[24] Langerbein says. The men assigned to carry out these brutal tasks began to show signs of struggling emotionally.

No Mercy for Infants

Concentration camps were places of appalling cruelty toward young children, especially infants. Most were killed immediately upon arrival. Female prisoners found to be pregnant were also killed; in some cases, however, they were kept alive so that cruel medical experiments could be performed to determine things like how long a newborn baby could survive without milk.

Women who were in the early stages of pregnancy when they arrived at the camps were sometimes able to disguise it, but pregnancy was a death sentence, and every day that passed increased the risk that a pregnancy would be noticed. Many pregnant women in the camps therefore opted to undergo painful forced abortions performed by fellow prisoners in the dark and without sterile tools.

Any infants delivered alive in the camps would be killed immediately and painfully if guards found them—some infants were thrown into fire pits while they were still alive. The mothers would die too, as punishment for hiding their pregnancy. Therefore, prisoners frequently killed newborns themselves by smothering them, drowning them in buckets of water, or giving lethal doses of morphine if they could obtain it. In the concentration camps, many prisoners considered killing infants quickly to be an act of mercy and also a way to spare the mother's life, at least for a while. In a concentration camp, there were no other choices.

The Nazis' answer to this problem was not to stop killing Jews or even to spare the children but just to carry out their murderous plot without forcing anyone to actually pull a trigger. The first of the hands-off killing methods took the form of trucks and vans into which groups of victims, after being ordered to undress, were herded. Once the doors were shut and locked behind the passengers, exhaust fumes from the truck's engine would be pumped into the back of the truck. People died horribly in the backs of the vans, often vomiting or losing control of their bladder in their last struggles for air.

When it was over, the vans were driven to grave sites so the bodies could be unloaded. Children's bodies were found intertwined with the limbs of parents, grandparents, siblings, or others who had tried to give them love and comfort in their final moments of consciousness. Sympathy for these smallest of victims had emotional effects on the Nazis who witnessed it firsthand while unloading the bodies, but it did nothing to slow the killing rampage of Hitler's regime. Trucks and vans, the new mobile murder units, replaced the gore of the firing squads but not the tragic circumstances of murdering children who wept and clung to their mothers and fathers or who had no one to cling to at all.

Factories of Death

Even as mobile killing squads terrorized victims with no regard for even the defenseless children among them, the Nazis were constructing still more-efficient killing facilities at concentration camps in Poland: Chelmno, Belzec, Sobibor, Treblinka, and especially Auschwitz-Birkenau, the most notorious killing center of them all. Nazi leaders no longer wanted to limit their victims to the number who could be crowded into the back of a truck or van. They devised and oversaw the construction of entire buildings designed to murder dozens of people at a time and thousands every day, with children being singled out before almost anyone else. In the words of Rudolf Höss, the commandant and chief overseer of Auschwitz, "Very young children, being incapable of working, were killed as a matter of principle." Not even their pleading mothers could save them. "Often women tried to hide their children under their clothes, but when they were found they were at once sent to their death,"[25] Höss said during war crimes trials after the war.

> "Very young children, being incapable of working, were killed as a matter of principle."[25]
>
> —Rudolf Höss, commandant of Auschwitz.

Carbon monoxide from exhaust fumes was effective for these indiscriminate mass killings, but not nearly as efficient as hydrogen cyanide, also known as prussic acid. In the 1920s German chemists

The walls inside the gas chamber at Majdanek concentration camp are stained blue from Zyklon B. Once exposed to air, Zyklon B pellets emitted deadly fumes. Those who breathed the fumes experienced vomiting, dizziness, and terror before they suffocated.

had discovered a way to use this powerful poison as a pesticide. They mass-produced their product in the form of pea-sized granules called Zyklon B and sold it in sealed metal canisters marked with a skull and crossbones to warn users about the risk of accidental poisoning. Zyklon B was widely used in World War II to disinfect buildings and ships and to kill pests. Initially it was used for the same purposes in concentration camps too. Almost every prisoner was afflicted with lice, and clothing had to be piled into special delousing rooms and treated with Zyklon B.

In time the Nazis noticed how much more effective the poison was against warm-blooded creatures like rats than against insects, and this realization led to a sinister new idea. By August 1941 the demand for Zyklon B in concentration camps increased considerably. The Nazis had begun using it to kill their camp prisoners by the millions, regarding them—and especially the children, who were sentenced to death more quickly than almost anyone—with no more compassion than they would a common rat.

Pellets of Zyklon B, when exposed to air, emit fumes of prussic acid, a deadly compound that has no color but smells like bitter almonds. Fumes enter the body through the skin, through mucous membranes such as the eyes, and especially through the lungs as the victim breathes. Once in the bloodstream, the acid prevents the body's cells from using oxygen. The victim eventually suffocates—but not before vomiting and experiencing dizziness and terror. Such was the fate of millions of people in the concentration camps.

Poisoning Children

From a child's point of view, the experience of entering a gas chamber must have been especially horrific. After traveling in overcrowded train cars to the concentration camp, the passengers would disembark only to be immediately assigned into one of two groups. Those who seemed strong and capable of working were sent one way. Those who were weak, sick, or elderly were put into another group, along with children, babies, and the mothers or other caretakers who accompanied them. These people were lined up in front of a long building and told to undress in preparation for a shower. Being nude in front of strangers was itself traumatic for children old enough to be aware of their surroundings, but the group of naked prisoners was then ordered to enter the building. They walked down cement steps and were crowded into a long room with a cement floor and walls. Several wire columns extended from floor to ceiling down the middle of the room. Some of these killing rooms still stand today, their walls bearing blue stains caused by chemical reactions between the cement and the prussic acid. The children who died in these rooms likely did not notice the stained walls in all the confusion.

Some of the adults being marched into the killing chambers knew or at least suspected that a shower was not the purpose of the room they were entering. Children likely absorbed the feelings of distress, despair, and panic in the adults around them as the doors were slammed shut behind them and locked. Once the doors were sealed, Nazi employees of the camps climbed to the roof of the building, put on gas masks, and dropped pellets of Zyklon B down chutes and into the room below. Within minutes the victims trapped in the killing chambers began to suffer the effects of the deadly gas. It took about fifteen minutes for all the victims in a gas chamber (as many as two hundred to three hundred at a time) to perish.

No one emerged from these chambers alive to tell about it. Men who were part of the Sonderkommando—camp prisoners (usually Jewish) forced to work in the killing chambers—provide some of the only existing accounts of the last moments of life for children who died this way. In the words of one anonymous member of the Sonderkommando, "Mothers march with small children in their arms; other children are now led by their tiny hands. . . . They want to go to their death together."[26]

> "Mothers march with small children in their arms; other children are now led by their tiny hands. . . . They want to go to their death together."[26]
>
> —An anonymous member of the Sonderkommando.

Marching Away from Freedom

While these dreadful events were happening in concentration camps, World War II raged on, and Germany was beginning to lose. By the summer of 1944 Russian forces were closing in on Poland and other German-occupied lands from the east, and British and American forces were advancing in the west. The Nazis realized their concentration camps would soon be discovered and the world would learn the truth about what had been taking place inside them.

The chief officers of camps in Poland received orders to destroy as much evidence of the killing as they could and to retreat to locations closer to Germany. The regularity of the gassing schedule and the cruel and mechanical routines at places like Auschwitz were replaced with chaos. To destroy evidence, Nazis used dynamite to blow up most of the gas chambers and crematoria (the buildings where bodies had been burned after they were removed from the gas chambers). There were still thousands of prisoners at Auschwitz, however, when Nazi leaders ordered it to be evacuated in the winter of 1944–1945. Lacking the time to kill all of these people and dispose of the bodies before the Russians arrived but afraid of all the secrets the prisoners would expose to the world if they were freed, the Nazis rounded up the surviving prisoners. Some of these people were loaded into trucks, wagons, or open train cars to transport them away from the camp. The rest were ordered to start walking. This was the start of what came to be known as the death marches of the Holocaust.

Because young children were almost always sent to gas chambers shortly after they arrived at the concentration camps, few remained to participate in the marches. Healthy older children, however, were often spared the gas chambers. Teenagers and children as young as ten or twelve joined the tens of thousands of prisoners forced to march away from the camps along snowy roads in the sub-zero January temperatures of Poland. Food was scarce—some might have had only some warm water and a piece of bread to sustain them for a day of

In the final days of World War II in Europe, the Nazis forced thousands of concentration camp prisoners—including young people—on death marches through the bleak, snow-covered countryside surrounding Auschwitz (pictured) and other camps.

Code Name T4

The Nazi regime had a vision of a racially pure society but also one with no genetic impurities—that is, a society in which no one had a disability that might be passed down to future generations. In this context, the Nazi regime singled out and killed people with a mental illness, learning disability, any kind of physical deformity, epilepsy, blindness, or deafness. The first such victims were residents of institutions for the physically or mentally disabled. The program then expanded to identify, early in life, individuals who suffered from disabilities Nazis believed would make them a burden on society.

In August 1939 the Nazi government decreed that all physicians, nurses, and midwives had to report any young people up to the age of seventeen who showed signs of a mental or physical disability, regardless of religious or ethnic background. Once reported, these children were segregated from society and killed either by starvation or a lethal overdose of medication. Even schoolteachers became part of the effort, reporting students whom they suspected might fit the criteria.

The policy of killing children with disabilities was masked by a code name, T4, named for the street address in Berlin (Tiergartenstrasse 4) where the program was headquartered. However, the number of physically and mentally disabled children killed as a result of the policy—estimated at a minimum of five thousand—was hard for the Nazis to hide. The murder of children who instead needed compassion and resources was one of the Holocaust's deepest outrages.

difficult hiking. Like other prisoners on these marches, the children lacked warm clothing like coats, gloves, or hats. Some had no shoes or only wooden clogs to walk in, and their feet left trails of blood in the snow.

In their quest to herd as many survivors as possible away from the camps, Nazi guards forced prisoners to walk many miles each day, showing no sympathy for either the old or the young. Those who stumbled or otherwise could not keep up were shot, their bodies often left by the side of the road for the other marchers to see as they passed. A woman named Mina who survived a Holocaust death march when she was sixteen recalls a terrible memory of the experience. "When I heard the echo of the shot at my mother, who was walking behind us in that death march, I was stricken dumb," she says. "I couldn't utter a sound. For more than a month I was unable to speak."[27] In the final weeks, days, and even hours before the concentration camps were discovered by Allied forces, the few children and teens lucky enough to have evaded death in the camps were, like Mina, forced to endure still more horrors. The lives of about one in four of the young people who embarked on death marches in the final days of Nazi control and terror were stopped in their tracks. The Nazis found ways to kill Jews until literally the final moments of the war.

CHAPTER FOUR

Escape and Rescue

Even though the Nazis hid their murderous activities in ghettos, concentration camps, and killing centers, people throughout Europe suspected that serious crimes were taking place. However, while World War II was devastating the Continent, governments, relief societies, and individuals were largely preoccupied with their own needs. Furthermore, anti-Semitism—hatred of Jews—was common, and so was fear of the Nazi regime, which promised swift and often deadly retribution for anyone who helped Jews.

Despite the chaotic and frightening circumstances in which the Holocaust took place, some people *were* willing to help, especially where young people were concerned. Both before and during the years of the Holocaust, people and organizations within and outside of Europe united in the effort to help Jewish children. Some did so openly, in defiance of the Nazis and their inhuman policies. Many others helped in secret, risking or even sacrificing their own lives or freedom to rescue young Jews and others. Without the efforts of these sympathetic people, the number of children murdered during the Holocaust would have been even higher.

An Urgency to Help

The Nazi regime achieved control of Germany in 1933. Years before the ghettos and camps, the radical anti-Semitic views of Adolf Hitler and his Nazi Party alarmed people all across Europe. European Jews, especially, sensed the coming of dreadful events. That same year Jews in Great Britain established a charity called the Central British Fund for German Jewry and began raising money to help Jews emigrate from Nazi-occupied areas.

Most people in the 1930s still seemed reluctant to believe that anti-Jewish hatred was reaching deadly levels, but events on the nights of November 9 and 10, 1938, served as proof that Jews in Germany truly were in terrible danger. On those nights, people throughout German territory engaged in violent anti-Jewish riots; they destroyed synagogues, businesses, and homes and beat up Jews in the streets. The rampage was known as Kristallnacht (Night of Broken Glass), and it demonstrated just how perilous life for Jews in Germany had become.

After Kristallnacht, the Central British Fund increased its fundraising efforts and its programs to help Jews escape Germany and reach Britain. The group made Jewish youth a priority. Margareta Burkill, a volunteer with the refugee movement, remembers how British citizens responded after Kristallnacht: "Every little town, every village in England said, 'We must save the children.' It was a fantastic thing."[28] Beginning in December 1938, Jewish parents throughout Germany and German-occupied lands raced to put their children's names on lists of individuals to whom Germans would grant safe passage to Britain. Over the next ten months, until World War II officially broke out in September 1939, approximately ten thousand Jewish children boarded trains and ships that would take them safely to the British Isles.

> "Every little town, every village in England said, 'We must save the children.' It was a fantastic thing."[28]
>
> —Margareta Burkill, a volunteer for a children's refugee movement.

Trains of Refuge

The British effort to rescue Jewish children was known as Kindertransport. In some ways the train cars crowded with children were a triumph because those aboard were to be spared the coming horrors of the ghettos and the concentration camps. However, the mood at the train stations and on the trains themselves was anything but jubilant. Each child clutched the single suitcase he or she was permitted to take. Somber families were allowed only a brief and tearful good-bye on the platform before the children were herded onto the passenger cars.

The sight of their mother and father waving from the platform as the train pulled away was, for many Kindertransport children, the last memory they would ever have of their parents. "I was all torn up inside," recalls a woman rescued by Kindertransport as a child. "It was really only when I looked out the window of the train and saw

Young German Jews who were whisked to safety by Kindertransport do their schoolwork in an English refugee camp in 1938. Some of the lucky few were reunited with family members after the war. Many never saw their families again.

my father standing there, totally frozen, that it hit me that I might never see him again. But by that time, it was too late to get back out of the train."[29] Children rescued by trains bound for England could not entirely outrun the tragedy of the Holocaust, which ultimately orphaned a majority of them.

Kindertransport was not the only program that gave refuge to Jewish children. Similar programs sponsored by Jewish organizations in France, Switzerland, and Spain helped as many as twelve thousand young people flee Nazi-occupied areas. The Jewish Agency in Jerusalem put together a movement called Youth Aliyah, which helped thousands more Jewish children escape to Palestine and Britain. However, there were limits to how many children could be rescued. Once the war began, host countries and families faced shortages in money, food, and other resources. Ambitious as the intentions of the rescue organizations were, they were ultimately hindered by the economic and social realities of a battle-torn continent. The tens of thousands of Jewish children saved through these programs was a small number compared to the millions who were never given the opportunity to flee.

Chosen but Not Blessed

In one of the great paradoxes of the Holocaust, young Jews considered lucky to have been rescued by transport did not always feel fortunate. Emotional shock, homesickness, and depression accompanied many of them on their journey to foreign lands. Most went to live with Jewish foster families who had agreed to take them in, but so many children needed homes that many non-Jewish families also stepped up to fill the need. Language barriers at first prevented any meaningful communication with new foster families and made it difficult for relocated youth to attend school and fit in. Meals, games, even clothing fashions differed from what was usual in the lives of the young Jews. Even children who joined Jewish families often faced a culture that had little in common with the one they had left behind. Those who ended up in Christian homes experienced an even larger divide between their familiar and treasured customs and those of their new life.

Like hidden children, the children of the Kindertransport and other rescue efforts faced a very difficult period of adjustment. "The English families who took care of me did the very best they could," Olga Levy Drucker remembers of her Kindertransport experience. "Under trying circumstances, they were enormously kind to me. . . . But because they were not my parents, they could not show me the love that I craved."[30] At first, displaced children like Olga clung to the belief that they would soon go home and be reunited with their parents. As the years went on, that hope began to dwindle. Older children, especially, came to understand that they were unlikely to see their families again. Programs like Kindertransport saved thousands of Jewish children's lives, but like most survival stories of the Holocaust, the victory was tainted by sorrow.

Rescued by the Underground

Organizations like the Central British Fund and Youth Aliyah came together to rescue Jewish children from afar. Another organization battled the Nazi abuses from the midst of where they were happening. In the heart of the ghettos and all across Nazi lands, a network of rebels formed a resistance movement known as the Underground. These rebels—many of whom were Jews, Gypsies, or members of other persecuted groups—despised Nazis and sought to thwart the abuses of the Holocaust in any way they could. Secretive Underground operatives, often disguised as guards or other workers loyal to the Nazi regime, carried out daring operations to smuggle children out of ghettos and other dangerous places.

The punishment for those caught helping Jews was death, and this limited the number of people who were willing to take an active role in the effort. Underground operatives could not stay long with the children they smuggled to safety because they had to return to help others. Furthermore, it usually was impossible for families to escape together because groups captured the attention of Nazi soldiers much more than a child here or there. Many children who escaped the Nazis therefore found themselves alone in a frightening world.

Danger was everywhere for a lone Jewish child. Nazi soldiers were always on the lookout for Jews, but there were also plenty of people willing to turn Jews over to the Nazis. The German government offered rewards for doing so. At a time when people had little money and little to eat, the promise of a reward often outweighed the guilt of turning in Jews—even children. Escaped children and teens quickly learned how to be suspicious, think quickly, lie convincingly, and run for their lives.

In the streets of cities, towns, and villages, escaped children became adept at passing themselves off as non-Jews who were just going about their daily business. Many obtained props to help with their act in case they were stopped and questioned. Girls might carry a basket of clothing or a loaf of bread, for example, so that they could claim they were paying a visit or running errands for a relative. Boys might carry an envelope or package and claim they were on their way to deliver it.

The best liars usually had the best chance of survival, but when lying failed, children knew they had to turn and run. They learned to scramble over fences and wriggle into abandoned buildings to evade Nazi soldiers or townspeople who wanted to turn them over to Nazis. "To me it was a game," says Joseph Steiner, who escaped from the Warsaw ghetto as a child. "Yes, people were killed, but I could never

A Bittersweet Ending

When Germany invaded Denmark in 1940, the Danes were unique in that their people, police force, and government actively resisted the Nazis' murderous intentions. Ultimately, Denmark's resistance was not enough to protect its Jews. Denmark was small, and Germany's military easily overpowered it. Determined to rescue as many of their Jewish citizens as possible, the Danes staged one of the greatest rescue efforts of the Holocaust. In the autumn of 1943 Danish fishermen and other citizens sneaked about seventy-two hundred Jews out of Denmark by boat to Sweden, which had agreed to harbor them until the war was over. Only about one hundred Danish Jews, or 1 percent of Denmark's Jewish population, were killed during the Holocaust, compared to about two-thirds of Jews from other German-occupied countries.

Denmark has long been a shining example of resistance to Nazi aggression, but not every Danish Jew found a happy ending. Silence was critical to smuggling Jews to safety by boat, and crying babies could have ruined the mission. Some parents of babies and young children fled to Sweden but left their children in Denmark with Christian caretakers. After the war ended, Jewish parents who returned to Denmark to reunite their families found that their young children had no memories of or attachment to them. Mothers and fathers faced the difficult decision of whether to pull their children away from loving foster parents or to let them be.

feel it. . . . I had no sense of reality. It was like a video game."[31] However, the stakes in this game were very high, as captured children were sent back to the ghettos or to concentration camps if they were not killed on the spot.

Many escaped children shunned the more populous towns and villages in favor of the countryside, where they were less likely to encounter Nazis or people who might turn them over to Nazis. However, life in the country was filled with its own gambles. Children often had to beg for food or shelter from strangers, never knowing who might turn them in. Most children who escaped the ghettos lived as transients—homeless, hungry, lonely, and wary of the dangers of getting caught.

Partisans in the Forests

In Poland and other parts of Nazi-occupied Europe, forests covered much of the landscape, and some escaped Jewish children tried to disappear among the trees. Winter was a brutal season in the forest, and many young people who ended up in this environment only survived by joining up with anti-Nazi bands who called themselves partisans. The goals of the partisans did not include comforting and sheltering children. The partisans often refused to let children live with them because they could not accept that added burden. The partisans oc-

Russian partisans attack a German military convoy. Jews in their teens who escaped the Nazis sometimes managed to join groups of partisans and resistance fighters. Because they were small, quick, and agile, they often served as messengers and lookouts.

casionally accepted boys and teenagers within their ranks, however, because they were more likely to help in the cause.

Poorly clothed and underfed, partisans often lived on carrots or potatoes stolen from farms at the outskirts of the woods, and they weathered the freezing, snowy winters in shelters made of logs and branches. "We lived in a hut . . . half underground and camouflaged with trees," says Ed Lessing, who escaped the Nazis and joined a partisan group when he was sixteen. "As the youngest person there and the only Jew, I wasn't welcomed with open arms, but I was tolerated."[32] The living conditions in the forests could be even more difficult than life in the ghettos, but with the partisans, boys like Ed could at least consider themselves free.

The partisans' goal was to wreak havoc on Nazis in any way possible. Most of these groups operated as guerrilla soldiers, small groups of fighters that ambush a larger, more organized, and better-equipped army. Partisans attacked Nazi camps, stole weapons, and blew up portions of Nazi railroads. Children and teens who joined partisan groups were expected to be useful, loyal members. Typically they served as lookouts and as members of reconnaissance groups, spying on Nazi soldiers to anticipate their next moves.

Child partisans were even given weapons and were expected to kill Nazis, if necessary, to protect the rest of the group. "I was so brainwashed that I totally believed it was either us or them; that the way they were dying they would do to you if they got you; and the more you kill of them the more likely it is that you stay alive," remembers a man who goes by Richard and who lived in the forest with a group of partisans as a child during the Holocaust. "I was already nine years old now, I understood clearly, and I was hardened by the previous sequence of events. I would have had no emotional problems shooting Germans from the tree because it was self-defence."[33] Accustomed to death and comfortable with the idea of killing to protect themselves, the boys and teenagers who lived in the forests with partisans were, like so many children of the Holocaust, robbed of the innocence of childhood in their daily struggle to survive.

> "I would have had no emotional problems shooting Germans from the tree because it was self-defence."[33]
>
> —Richard, a child member of a partisan group.

Laboring to Survive

Young Jewish children captured by Nazis during the Holocaust typically faced swift and brutal death, but Jewish teenagers were often forced to work as slaves. They were sent all over German territory, usually to perform difficult manual labor. Many teenage workers helped provide raw materials for the Nazis' massive construction projects, laboring in stone quarries or brick factories. Others worked in factories to produce war supplies. Some were assigned to help construct new concentration camps or were even forced to work in the killing centers of the camps, doing jobs like digging mass graves and hauling corpses out of gas chambers and into the crematoria to be incinerated.

The young workers were underfed and faced constant abuse and humiliation. The Nazis did not mind (in fact, they preferred) if slave laborers, even those as young as ten or eleven, died from starvation or were worked to death. Despite the horrific and often deadly conditions, labor became a survival strategy for some young prisoners. Those who showed willingness to work not only avoided the gas chambers but also usually obtained slightly more food than other prisoners. Far more working teenagers survived the Holocaust than younger children, most of whom the Nazis immediately sentenced to die.

Above the gates of Auschwitz are the infamous words *Arbeit Macht Frei*: "Work makes one free." The Nazis had no real intention of freeing prisoners, but hard work ultimately did see some teenagers through the Holocaust to liberation.

Liberation

Whether they were trapped in ghettos or concentration camps, evading Nazis in towns or cities, or living with partisans in the forests, persecuted youth were often too preoccupied with survival to know or understand that World War II was coming to an end. The Allies—the combined forces of Russia, Britain, and the United States—eventually closed in on and overpowered Nazi Germany and its territories. On May 8, 1945, Germany surrendered to the Allies, and the war in Europe was over.

After years of living in fear and hiding, Jews and other groups that had been tormented by Nazis slowly began to emerge. They crept out of abandoned buildings, bunkers, basements, and underground sewers in the cities. They walked out of forests or away from barns and fields in the countryside. They took shaky steps (or had to be carried) through the gates of ghettos and concentration camps, opened by Russian, British, and American soldiers for the first time in years. "We just crawled out of our hiding places and were happy about our newly regained freedom," says Gert Silberbart, who at age seventeen was among the prisoners liberated from the Buchenwald concentration

Jubilant young prisoners of the Dachau concentration camp cheer the arrival of the US Army in May 1945. Some liberated prisoners could barely stand or walk, but all cherished their newfound freedom.

camp. Although he managed to walk out to greet the American soldiers, he says, "I was too weak to just go a few steps. . . . I just rested."[34]

Four hundred miles (644 km) away at Auschwitz, Eva Mozes Kor and her twin sister had miraculously survived medical experiments to see liberation. "I kept peering through the snow, and finally I saw them—the Soviet Army, wearing all white camouflage outfits, were approaching Auschwitz I," she remembers. "We ran out and everybody was hugging and kissing and shouting, 'We are free. We are free.'"[35] The Nazis' reign of terror was over. The surviving Jews, Gypsies, and other victims were released.

> "We just crawled out of our hiding places and were happy about our newly regained freedom."[34]
>
> —Gert Silberbart, a teenage survivor of Buchenwald.

However, the children among them bore deep scars, both physical and emotional. They had learned to be timid and had been forced into a life of fear. The future they faced was not one of celebration but of new kinds of struggles.

CHAPTER FIVE

Growing Up After the Holocaust

With the end of World War II came the liberation of the people trapped in concentration camps and ghettos. Although the war's end was a time of relief and celebration, it also brought to light the horrific abuses the Nazis had inflicted on their victims. Soldiers and government officials from Russia, Britain, and the United States toured the remains of the concentration camps and were sobered by the extent of the blatant violence and torture evident in their midst. Despite the Nazis' attempts to cover up their brutality, they could not silence the hellish stories of the survivors, which might have seemed like insane ranting if not for the physical condition of the people still alive in the camps and the piles of bodies unearthed from mass graves. "The sight that met our startled gaze was enough to bring forth a censorable exclamation from a sergeant who has seen the bloodiest fighting this war has offered," US Army major Cameron Coffman reported after Allied forces liberated one of the smaller concentration camps. "Row upon row of living skeletons, jammed so closely together that it was impossible for some to turn over, even if they could have generated enough strength to do so, met our eyes."[36]

Some of the most shocking and disturbing evidence found in the camps proved that a staggering number of children and babies had been subjected to the Nazis' extermination campaign. Tiny shirts, pants, and dresses were discovered among the piles of clothing confiscated from people who had been murdered in the camps. At Auschwitz-Birkenau, now a World Heritage Site and the most visited Holocaust memorial in the world, a bin displays thousands of pairs of children's shoes that were recovered after the Soviets liberated the camp on January 27, 1945. There were not, however, thousands of children alive in the camp to reclaim the shoes. The haunting truth was evident—the young owners of those small shoes would never be seen again.

In the aftermath of such profound tragedy, freedom rang through Germany and the rest of Nazi territory like a hollow echo. The end of war brought relief to most European citizens, and they were eager to put their troubles behind them and return to life as they knew it. Jewish, Gypsy, and other persecuted families, however, had been torn apart during the war and in the years that led up to it. Mending what remained of those families meant locating and bringing together survivors scattered across the Continent. Children and teens separated from their parents during the Holocaust faced some of their most significant struggles once the war was over. European society seemed to expect them to go home, but after so many years of persecution and hiding, many had no concept of where or even what home was.

Camps for the Displaced

Children and teens who had lived in camps or ghettos or who had survived the war by hiding in fields or forests were gradually collected and sent to camps built—or, in the case of some former concentration camps, ironically repurposed—as holding areas for displaced persons (DPs). These camps lacked barbed-wire fences and guards. Food, medical care, and other important resources were plentiful there. However, living in barracks-style shelters was still a necessity because the number of DPs was overwhelming. Approximately one million people spent at least some time in such camps between the end of the war and 1952. Among the residents were many children who had nowhere to go and no one to look after them. "We had a difficult time dealing with freedom," says Kuba Beck, a young woman who survived the Holocaust as a teenager and entered a Polish DP camp with her sister after the war. "There was no fanfare, no family to return to, no country to speak for us."[37]

> "We had a difficult time dealing with freedom. There was no fanfare, no family to return to, no country to speak for us."[37]
>
> —Kuba Beck, a young woman in a displaced persons camp.

A main goal of the DP camps was to reunite family members who had lost touch with each other during the war. Records were made of every resident's name and other identifying information, and the various camps shared this information with radio stations and news-

Young boys await an uncertain future at a displaced persons camp in 1946 in Berlin. Thousands of children and teens who survived the Holocaust were sent to DP camps, where workers desperately tried to help them reunite with their families.

papers in the hope of connecting relatives who had lost one another. However, children brought to the camps had often been taken from their parents or other family members when they were too young to know their own name, or their birth names had since been changed by the people looking after them to mask their Jewishness. Countless families' histories, records, and photographs had been lost or destroyed during the war, making the task of matching lost children with family members even more challenging.

Stolen Children

As Germany occupied various countries, Nazi soldiers were instructed to look for young children with blond hair and blue eyes—those who fit the description of people with whom Hitler wanted to populate the Continent. If an SS soldier spied such a child in an occupied country, he was entitled to kidnap him or her. Captured children were taken back to Germany to undergo a racial assessment. Those who did not pass were usually sent to children's homes or forced-labor camps. Those who passed were distributed to German mothers and fathers who wanted to raise them. The children were Germanized, or brought up to believe they were German.

An estimated fifty thousand to two hundred thousand children from Poland and other countries were kidnapped by SS soldiers for this purpose. Often the stolen children were listed by Nazis as having been orphaned, but in reality the SS soldiers had usually killed the child's parents or sent them off to concentration camps. After the war some countries demanded that their stolen children be returned to them, but the German parents who adopted these children rarely gave them up. The children themselves had often been too young when they were taken to realize that they were not German and therefore did not protest. The theft and relocation of children based on their appearance alone left its own legacy of loss after the Holocaust.

Parents who survived the Holocaust searched for their sons and daughters, but many children had either no recollection or only a few vague memories of their real mother and father. The reverse was also true—children who did remember their parents and siblings and longed to find them were often confronted with the terrible reality that family members had not survived or that no one knew what had become of them. Many of these children were destined to spend the rest of their lives wondering, hoping, and yearning. "One never stops searching for relatives that have vanished, even if one burrows only in one's soul,"[38] says Joseph Berger, the son of two Holocaust survivors.

Children Reclaimed

While some children and teenagers waited in DP camps to find adult relatives who could care for them, many others still lived with foster families, often in countries outside Germany, Poland, or other areas the Nazis had heavily scoured for Jews. Some children had bounced from one foster home or orphanage to another, changing locations whenever the Nazis got too close. This made it difficult for surviving parents or other relatives to find children after the war. They often had to follow a frustrating trail of clues to track down children who were no longer where they had been left.

Parents who did succeed in finding their children after the Holocaust sometimes faced an unexpected outcome: Their child had formed strong bonds with his or her foster family or caretakers. The return of a long-lost mother or father after the war was supposed to be a happy ending for both parent and child, but children who had been in loving homes for years often shunned their birth parents and wanted to stay with the people they knew. "I remember sitting in the kitchen crying and screaming that I didn't want to go back to my mother,"[39] says Basia Bonnewit, a child hidden with a foster family during the Holocaust.

> "One never stops searching for relatives that have vanished, even if one burrows only in one's soul."[38]
>
> —Joseph Berger, the son of Holocaust survivors.

The dream of being reunited with children they had left behind had helped many parents survive in ghettos, concentration camps, or on the run. It was devastating when the long-anticipated joy of returning for their children did not turn out the way they had hoped. A woman named Mira, who was hidden as a young child during the Holocaust, remembers the struggle to give love when her mother came back for her: "She looked very different. But it was clearly my mother. Yet for years after the war I had this fantasy that I was adopted, that my parents weren't my real parents."[40] The Holocaust forced heartbreak on many Jewish families twice. Parents and children were first wrenched apart in the effort to save themselves, and later they had to accept the painful reality that years of separation made it difficult or impossible for things to go back to the way they had been.

An Exodus from Europe

Children reunited with their parents, siblings, aunts or uncles, or other relatives after the Holocaust still faced great uncertainty and upheaval in its aftermath. The Nazis had taken away Jews' homes, jobs, money, and valuables, leaving Jewish parents who survived the war jobless, penniless, and with nowhere to take their children. Now that the war was over and the Nazis' reign of terror was no longer a looming threat, nations throughout Europe began to close their doors to homeless Jewish families who were still very much in need of money, shelter, and kindness. Their former homes, in most cases, had either been destroyed or were now occupied by new residents who were unwilling to give them back. The war was over, but the plight of Europe's surviving Jews seemed never ending.

Organizations like the Jewish Joint Distribution Committee and the Hebrew Immigrant Aid Society raised money to help European Jews travel to and settle in new places such as the United States, Israel, Canada, and South Africa. Communities of Jewish refugees developed all over the world. In new cities, new homes, and new lives, thousands of Jewish children once more found themselves in strange and foreign circumstances. Many were still adjusting to life with parents, aunts and uncles, or other relatives from whom they had been separated for years. Now they also had to adjust to life in a foreign place, often where people spoke another language and where cultural customs were unfamiliar.

People underestimated the difficulty Jewish children had after the Holocaust and after immigrating to different countries. Many of these children had been deprived of a formal education for years while in ghettos or in hiding and could not read or write in their native language, much less in the new language they had to learn. They were often very poor and were frequently bullied or shunned by their peers at school. Anti-Semitism still existed.

On top of these challenges, many Jewish children also bore the weight of traumatic memories of abuse and violence they had seen or endured during the Holocaust. Jewish parents themselves had witnessed unspeakable things during the Holocaust years. The memories left many of them either emotionally closed off from their own children or overly protective to the point of smothering them. Children and teens who endured the Holocaust and its turbulent aftermath carried burdens most other people could not comprehend. Yet they

A ship carrying Jewish Holocaust survivors docks at the port of Haifa in 1947 in the British mandate of Palestine (now Israel). Adjusting to life in Israel, the United States, and other countries presented many challenges for refugees—young and old.

were often expected or even told to feel fortunate that they had survived, as Nicole David recalls:

> When I would talk about the war, the food, the bombing, whatever, people would say: what do you *mean* about the war; you're lucky, you survived. . . . But I always say to people: this is not what it's about. It's about understanding how people survived during the war, about the *whole* story of the Holocaust: that besides the camps, there was the fear of having to find hiding places, of how to hide, the separation from parents, of not having a childhood, not having had a youth. . . . We are the youngest survivors of the Holocaust, our story is part of the full story.[41]

Reaching Adulthood

Despite the struggles survivors faced, the Holocaust had taught them to be resilient and develop coping mechanisms to make life tolerable. "For the most part, the refugees went about trying to create the same prosaic lives for themselves that their working-class neighbors had," says Berger. "They had to find jobs, learn their way around the subways, choose schools, provide music and dance lessons, and steer their children into productive lives."[42] In the decades after the Holocaust, many of its youngest survivors pursued higher education, married, and raised families of their own. Some never went back to their native country, but others returned to visit or even to live there. Many hidden children kept in touch with the foster families who had given them shelter.

> "We are the youngest survivors of the Holocaust, our story is part of the full story."[41]
>
> —Nicole David, a child survivor.

Over time, support groups developed for children who survived the Holocaust. In Europe, the United States, and elsewhere, those living with the memories of this dark period still come together to share stories or just to have a sense of belonging with others who truly understand. The World Federation of Jewish Child Survivors of the Holocaust and Descendants holds events for survivors, as does the

A Timeless Photograph

On January 27, 1945, Russian military forces liberated the 2,819 surviving prisoners of the Auschwitz-Birkenau concentration camp. Only 180 survivors were children or teenagers. A photographer took a picture of thirteen of these children, dressed in striped prisoner garb and standing in the snow behind a barbed-wire fence. The photograph has since become an iconic image of the Holocaust.

On January 27, 2015, the seventieth anniversary of the camp's liberation, four of the children in the photograph returned to Auschwitz to take part in a Holocaust memorial and remembrance service there. They had been identified and located by a California-based genocide research institute called the Shoah Foundation. Organized by American film director Steven Spielberg, whose movies include the 1993 Oscar-winning Holocaust film *Schindler's List*, the Shoah Foundation has created a living history database of audiovisual interviews with almost fifty-two thousand survivors of the Holocaust and other genocides. "The testimonies help others hear stories that are not easy to tell or listen to," says Spielberg, who is Jewish.

The stories of the four survivors from the 1945 photograph are among those the Shoah Foundation has been able to preserve. Miriam Friedman Ziegler, identifiable in the picture because she was revealing the prisoner number tattooed on her forearm, is grateful for the chance to share her story. "I was lucky enough to live," she says. "I want the world to know."

Quoted in Sherry Amatenstein, "'This Is What I Was Put on Earth to Do'—Steven Spielberg," *USA Weekend*, April 30, 2014. http://experience.usatoday.com.

Quoted in Liam Casey, "Auschwitz Survivor Living in Canada Returning for Liberation Anniversary," CTV News Canada, January 25, 2015. www.ctvnews.ca.

Hidden Child Foundation. Attendees at such gatherings represent a living repository of the effects of persecution and hatred but also of healing and hope.

Many of those who experienced the Holocaust as children have come forward to tell, share, and publish their stories. Among the famous child survivors of the Holocaust is Polish-born film director Roman Polanski. Polanski spent the Holocaust years hiding with Catholic peasants to evade the Nazis, who had sent both his parents to concentration camps and murdered his mother at Auschwitz. As a boy Polanski often hid in movie theaters to escape the attention of Nazis, and he later grew up to make movies of his own—usually chilling psychological thrillers like *Rosemary's Baby* in 1968 and *Chinatown* in 1974. In 2002 he made *The Pianist*, a film adapted from the autobiography of Warsaw ghetto survivor Wladyslaw Szpilman. The film won three Academy Awards, including best director. It gave Polanski a unique opportunity to chronicle a story of the Holocaust as authentically as only a man who had once lived through it could.

Another child survivor has become a globally renowned advocate of human rights. Elie Wiesel, who survived internment at Auschwitz when he was fifteen, has written widely about the Holocaust. His internationally acclaimed memoir *Night* has become standard reading in many high schools. He moved to the United States in 1956, and in 1978 he was appointed chair of the President's Commission on the Holocaust by Jimmy Carter. In 1980 he became the founding chair of the US Holocaust Memorial Council. A devoted teacher, he holds honorary degrees from more than one hundred universities and has been a professor at Yale University, Boston University, and the City University of New York. He was awarded the Nobel Peace Prize in 1986 for his worldwide humanitarian efforts.

Like all child survivors who have spoken out about their experiences, people like Wiesel and Polanski have been instrumental in keeping the Holocaust from falling into the fog of past memories. However, as Wiesel points out, the testaments of child survivors have sometimes come at a cost:

> After the war, most of the survivors did in fact refuse to speak. . . . Our guilt derives now from the feeling that perhaps we should not have spoken at all, especially in the light of some of the vulgarity that surrounds this theme today. The Holocaust has suddenly become a fashionable subject, a household word. . . . Because we did succeed, at least in part, to create a certain awareness of the Holocaust, others began to misuse the subject, misunderstand, misinterpret, and distort it.[43]

Students at a Florida school listen with rapt attention to the stories of men and women who experienced the Holocaust as children. Many aging survivors have come forward to share their stories so that future generations never forget the evils that took place during the Holocaust.

Survivors' words alone may never be able to convey the full truth of the Holocaust to those who were not there, as Wiesel has often expressed. Nevertheless, the child survivors who have spoken out, each in his or her own way, have helped keep the memories of the Holocaust and its victims from being buried by the passage of time.

Receding History

The youngest of the Holocaust survivors are now among the only survivors still alive. More survivors pass away each year. Someday soon there will be no more eyewitnesses, no more testimonies or first-person accounts to be shared. The time remaining to bring these stories to light is short. Many survivors, now growing old, feel a need to share their own memories of the Holocaust as it was experienced by its youngest and most innocent victims. "We learn from our experience as

Hidden Children that when ordinary citizens take a stand and refuse to give in to evil, the miracle of survival can occur," says Abraham H. Foxman, national director of the Anti-Defamation League and himself a hidden child during the Holocaust. "As we move further away from the Holocaust, our story of moral integrity and courage is that much more relevant and poignant. Our mission is to educate future generations so that no people, no nation, may again suffer the evil of the Holocaust."[44]

> "The survivors are calling out to us from the depths of their hearts, 'please keep the memory alive.'"[45]
>
> —Rabbi Ephraim Mirvis.

When history reflects on the Holocaust, it can gain no purer perspective than to view the events through the stories and eyes of the children who were there and have been brave enough to speak of the past. "The survivors are calling out to us from the depths of their hearts," said Rabbi Ephraim Mirvis on the seventieth anniversary of the liberation of Auschwitz-Birkenau on January 27, 2015, "'please keep the memory alive.'"[45]

SOURCE NOTES

Introduction: Children Deemed Less than Human

1. Quoted in Norman Rose, *Chaim Weizmann: A Biography*. New York: Penguin, 1986, p. 354.

2. Quoted in Paul R. Mendes-Flohr and Jehuda Reinharz, eds., *The Jew in the Modern World: A Documentary History*. New York: Oxford University Press, 1995, p. 684.

3. Quoted in US Holocaust Memorial Museum, "Plight of Jewish Children," *Holocaust Encyclopedia*. www.ushmm.org.

Chapter One: Children in Hiding

4. Quoted in Jeanne Manning, *A Time to Speak*. Paducah, KY: Turner, 1999, p. 510.

5. Chaya H. Roth, *The Fate of Holocaust Memories: Transmission and Family Dialogues*. New York: Palgrave MacMillan, 2008, p. 76.

6. Nechama Tec, *Dry Tears: The Story of a Lost Childhood*. Westport, CT: Wildcat, 1982, p. 144.

7. Olga Kirshenbaum Weiss, "Reminiscences of Being Hidden," in *Out of Chaos: Hidden Children Remember the Holocaust*, ed. Elaine Saphier Fox. Evanston, IL: Northwestern University Press, 2013, p. 62.

8. Quoted in Paul Valent, *Child Survivors of the Holocaust*. New York: Brunner-Routledge, 2002, p. 58.

9. Ilana Rosen, *Sister in Sorrow: Life Histories of Female Holocaust Survivors from Hungary*. Detroit: Wayne State University Press, 2008, pp. 179–80.

10. Ingrid Epstein Elefant, *A Time of Silence: The Story of a Childhood Holocaust Survivor*. Bloomington, IN: AuthorHouse, 2011, p. 41.

11. Quoted in Sara R. Horowitz, "'If He Knows to Make a Child. . . .': Memories of Birth and Baby-Killing in Deferred Jewish Testimony Narratives," in *Jewish Histories of the Holocaust: New Transnational Approaches*, ed. Norman J.W. Goda. Oxford, NY: Berghahn, 2014, p. 139.

12. Quoted in Jill Martin, *Surviving the Holocaust.* Seattle: Amazon Digital Services, 2014. Kindle edition.

13. Robert Krell, "Child Survivors of the Holocaust," in *Child Holocaust Survivors: Memories and Reflections,* by Robert Krell et al. Bloomington, IN: Trafford, 2007, p. 115.

Chapter Two: Children in Captivity

14. Emanuel Ringelblum, *Notes from the Warsaw Ghetto,* ed. Jacob Sloan. New York: Shocken, 1974, p. 223.

15. Anne Maxwell, *Picture Imperfect: Photography and Eugenics, 1870–1940.* Portland, OR: Sussex Academic, 2008, p. 261.

16. Quoted in Rupert Butler, *Legions of Death: The Nazi Enslavement of Europe.* Yorkshire, UK: Pen & Sword, 2004. EBook edition, chap. 5.

17. Quoted in Diane Plotkin, "Smuggling in the Ghettos," in *Life in the Ghettos During the Holocaust,* ed. Eric Sterling. Syracuse, NY: Syracuse University Press, 2004, p. 92.

18. Quoted in Nancy R. Goodman and Marilyn B. Meyers, eds., *The Power of Witnessing: Reflections, Reverberations, and Traces of the Holocaust.* New York: Routledge, 2012, p. 335.

19. Quoted in Serge Klarsfeld, *French Children of the Holocaust: A Memorial.* New York: Beate Klarsfeld Foundation, 1996, p. 91.

20. Quoted in Laurence Rees and Catherine Tatge, directors, "Factories of Death," episode 4 of *Auschwitz: The Nazis and the Final Solution,* BBC Worldwide, 2005. www.bbc.co.uk.

21. Quoted in Rees and Tatge, "Factories of Death."

Chapter Three: The Killing of Children

22. Eve Nussbaum Soumerai and Carol D. Schulz, *Daily Life During the Holocaust.* Westport, CT: Greenwood, 2009, p. 148.

23. Quoted in Richard Rhodes, *Masters of Death: The SS-Einsatzgruppen and the Invention of the Holocaust.* New York: Knopf, 2002, p. 135.

24. Helmut Langerbein, *Hitler's Death Squads: The Logic of Mass Murder*. College Station: Texas A&M University Press, 2004, pp. 39, 58.

25. Quoted in Norbert Ehrenfreund, *The Nuremberg Legacy: How the Nazi War Crimes Trials Changed the Course of History*. New York: Palgrave MacMillan, 2007, p. 44.

26. Quoted in Gideon Greif, *We Wept Without Tears: Testimonies of the Jewish Sonderkommando from Auschwitz*. New Haven, CT: Yale University Press, 2005, p. 26.

27. Quoted in Dina Wardip, *Memorial Candles: Children of the Holocaust*. New York: Routledge, 2013, p. 11.

Chapter Four: Escape and Rescue

28. Quoted in Vera K. Fast, *Children's Exodus: A History of the Kindertransport*. London: Taurus, 2011, pp. 13–14.

29. Quoted in Sue Read, director, "The Children Who Cheated the Nazis." London: Golden Reed Productions, 2001. Video. www.amazon.com/Children-Who-Cheated-Nazis/dp/B00R GV0CR2/ref=sr_1_1?ie=UTF8&qid=1426547634&sr=8-1&key words=The+Children+Who+Cheated+the+Nazis.

30. Olga Levy Drucker, *Kindertransport*. New York: Holt, 1992, p. 145.

31. Quoted in Martin, *Surviving the Holocaust*.

32. Quoted in Martin, *Surviving the Holocaust*.

33. Quoted in Valent, *Child Survivors of the Holocaust*.

34. Quoted in Patricia Heberer, *Children During the Holocaust*. Plymouth, UK: AltaMira, 2011, p. 380.

35. Quoted in John J. Michalczyk, *Filming the End of the Holocaust: Allied Documentaries, Nuremberg and the Liberation of the Concentration Camps*. New York: Bloomsbury Academic, 2014, p. 59.

Chapter Five: Growing Up After the Holocaust

36. Quoted in Hugo Gryn and Naomi Gryn, *Chasing Shadows*. New York: Penguin, 2001, p. 262.

37. Kuba Beck and Helen Beck, "Two Saved by Schindler," in *And Life Is Changed Forever: Holocaust Childhoods Remembered*, ed. Martin Ira Glassner and Robert Krell. Detroit: Wayne State University Press, 2006, p. 222.

38. Quoted in Nancy Nemeth-Jesurun, *The Third Life: Sixteen Holocaust Survivors in El Paso*. Ann Arbor, MI: ProQuest, 2008, p. 245.

39. Quoted in Kerry Bluglass, *Hidden from the Holocaust: Stories of Resilient Children Who Survived and Thrived*. Santa Barbara, CA: Praeger, 2003, p. 187.

40. Quoted in Lawrence L. Langer, *Using and Abusing the Holocaust*. Bloomington: Indiana University Press, 2006, p. 65.

41. Quoted in Lyn Smith and the Imperial War Museum, *Forgotten Voices of the Holocaust: True Stories of Survival—from Men, Women, and Children Who Were There*. London: Ebury, 2005, p. 330.

42. Joseph Berger, *Displaced Persons: Growing Up American After the Holocaust*. New York: Washington Square, 2001, p. 17.

43. Elie Wiesel, *Elie Wiesel: Conversations*. Jackson: University Press of Mississippi, 2002, pp. 53–54.

44. Abraham H. Foxman, "The Message of the Holocaust's 'Hidden Children,'" Anti-Defamation League, August 27, 2003. http://archive.adl.org.

45. Quoted in Caroline Davies, "Holocaust Survivors Call Out 'Please Keep the Memory Alive,' Says Chief Rabbi," *Guardian* (Manchester), January 27, 2015. www.theguardian.com.

Joseph André

(1908–1973) A Catholic priest in Belgium who found safe homes for hundreds of Jewish children. He encouraged children to keep practicing their Jewish faith.

Anne Frank

(1929–1945) A teenaged Jewish diarist who chronicled her experience of hiding in an Amsterdam office building from 1942 to 1944. She died in a concentration camp. *Anne Frank: The Diary of a Young Girl*, first published in 1947, has been translated into sixty-seven languages.

Janusz Korczak

(1878–1942) A Polish Jew, pediatrician, and children's author who operated an orphanage for Jewish children in the Warsaw ghetto. Refusing several chances to escape, he ultimately died with his two hundred orphans at the Treblinka concentration camp.

Josef Mengele

(1911–1979) An SS physician at Auschwitz who conducted often deadly medical experiments on children, especially twins. He fled to South America after the war to escape prosecution for his crimes.

Yvonne Névejean

(1900–1987) The head of a Belgian agency that gave new identities and permanent places of refuge to more than four thousand Jewish children. The young people she saved were known as "Yvonne's children."

Emanuel Ringelblum

(1900–1944) A relief worker who compiled thousands of historically priceless records and documents from within the Warsaw ghetto, many describing experiences of children. He was executed in the ghetto.

Baldur von Schirach

(1907–1974) Schirach earned great fame when appointed by Hitler as youth leader of the German Reich. He participated in deporting Austrian Jews to ghettos but fell out of favor with the Nazi government for criticizing its harsh treatment of Jews. He served twenty years in prison for crimes against humanity.

Irena Sendler

(1910–2008) A Polish social worker who smuggled nearly twenty-five hundred Jewish children out of the Warsaw ghetto to homes, orphanages, and convents. She kept records and later tracked many of them down to reunite them with their real families.

Miriam Wattenberg

(1924–2013) A Jewish Warsaw ghetto captive who started a journal at age fifteen. First published in 1945 under the pen name Mary Berg, the diary was one of very few eyewitness accounts of the Warsaw ghetto.

Elie Wiesel

(1928–) A teen survivor of Auschwitz who grew up to become a political activist and a prolific author. *Night*, his memoir of life in a concentration camp, has been translated into thirty languages. He was awarded the Nobel Peace Prize in 1986.

Books

Linda Jacobs Altman, *Hidden Teens, Hidden Lives: Primary Sources from the Holocaust*. New York: Enslow, 2010.

Ann Byers, *Saving Children from the Holocaust: The Kindertransport*. New York: Enslow, 2012.

Susan Brophy Down, *Irena Sendler: Bringing Life to Children of the Holocaust*. New York: Crabtree, 2012.

Anne Frank, *Anne Frank: The Diary of a Young Girl*. 1947. Reprint, New York: Doubleday, 2008.

Laurel Holliday, *Children in the Holocaust and World War II: Their Secret Diaries*. New York: Pocket, 2014.

Marcel Prins and Peter Henk Steenhuis, *Hidden Like Anne Frank: 14 True Stories of Survival*. New York: Levine, 2014.

Andrea Warren, *Surviving Hitler: A Boy in the Nazi Death Camps*. New York: HarperCollins, 2013.

Elie Wiesel, *Night*, trans. Marion Wiesel. 1972. Reprint, New York: Hill and Wang, 2006.

Internet Sources

Allan Hall, "The Little Ones That Got Away: Incredible Stories of Jewish Children Who Survived the Nazi Holocaust," *Daily Mail* (London), March 23, 2013. www.dailymail.co.uk/news/article-2298027/The-little-ones-got-away-Incredible-stories-Jewish-children-survived-Nazi-holocaust.html.

Robert Hardman, "The Children of Auschwitz: On the Eve of the 70th Anniversary of Its Liberation, Jews Who Appeared as Youngsters in Photograph Taken at the Concentration Camp Join Those Revisiting Their Past," *Daily Mail* (London), January 26, 2015. www.dailymail.co.uk/news/article-2926645/Survivors-visit-Auschwitz-day-ahead-70th-anniversary.html.

Time Life, "'50 Children': An American Couple's Mission to Save Kids from the Third Reich." http://life.time.com/history/50-children -an-american-couple-saves-kids-from-nazi-germany/#1.

Websites

Hidden Child Foundation (http://archive.adl.org/hidden/default .html). Part of the Anti-Defamation League, this organization was founded in 1931 to combat anti-Semitism, support children of the Holocaust, and provide educational resources. It offers firsthand accounts of the experiences of hidden children, discussion guides, information about gatherings and conferences, and links for hidden children or descendants who are searching for loved ones.

Project Aladdin (www.projetaladin.org/holocaust/en/muslims-and -jews/muslims-and-jews-in-history/muslims-and-jews-in-history .html). Project Aladdin provides a background of the Holocaust with first-person accounts and videos. It includes a page devoted to children's Holocaust experiences and a free online library of books and other resources.

Teacher's Guide to the Holocaust (http://fcit.coedu.usf.edu/ho locaust/people/children.htm). This site, hosted by the Florida Center for Instructional Technology at the University of South Florida, provides a thorough overview of the Holocaust through photographs, documents, art, music, movies, and literature for classroom use. It includes a page devoted to children with sections on hidden children, the Kindertransport, and the Hitler Youth, and links to documents, websites, first-person accounts, and videos.

US Holocaust Memorial Museum (www.ushmm.org). America's national institution for the study of Holocaust history. Its searchable website features thousands of videos, images, articles, audio files, first-person accounts, and other resources describing the experiences of children.

World Federation of Jewish Child Survivors of the Holocaust and Descendants (www.holocaustchild.org). The federation represents and brings together Jews who survived the Holocaust as children. It provides resources for students and educators, survivor stories, and a way to contact survivors.

INDEX

Jenny MacKay has written thirty books for teens and preteens on topics ranging from crime scene investigation and technological marvels to historical issues and the science of sports. She lives in Sparks, Nevada.

5